JOIN THE SINNERS AND SAINTS NETWORKING CLUB

As you turn the final page of "The 7 Deadly Sins of Networking," your journey does not have to end here. In fact, a new chapter awaits you – one that involves becoming part of a vibrant, engaging, and supportive community. We invite you to join the Sinners and Saints Networking Club on LinkedIn, a community dedicated to transforming the way we network, one connection at a time.

What to Expect in the Community:

- Continuous Learning: Just like the stories and lessons in the book, our community is a space for ongoing learning and development. Engage in discussions, share insights, and gain new perspectives on effective networking.

- Real-World Application: Apply the virtues of Humility, Gratitude, Temperance, Chastity, Patience, Generosity, and Diligence in real-world scenarios. Share your experiences and learn how others are integrating these principles into their professional lives.

- Supportive Network: Connect with like-minded professionals who are also on a journey to improve their networking skills. Find mentors, collaborators, and friends who can support you in your professional growth.

- Interactive Challenges and Activities: Participate in challenges and activities designed to help you practice the virtues in practical, everyday situations.

- Expert Guidance: Gain insights from industry experts, join webinars, and participate in Q&A sessions to deepen your understanding of effective networking.
- Community Engagement: Share your successes and challenges, ask for advice, and offer your support to others. This club is about mutual growth and collective success.

Your Next Step in Networking Excellence

Joining the Sinners and Saints Networking Club is more than just being part of a group; it is about being part of a movement that values authentic, meaningful, and effective networking. It is a place where the lessons from the book come to life, and where you can continue to grow, learn, and succeed.

We cannot wait to welcome you into our community. Together, let us turn networking sins into networking wins!

You can learn more by visiting us at

https://www.globalwellnesshq.com/sinners-and-saints-networking-club

The 7 Deadly Sins of Networking And The 7 Redeeming Virtues

A Business Parable About Business Networking And How To Redeem Yourself When You Fall From Grace

Jeff Borschowa

Published by Pharos Business Services Inc.
Edmonton, Alberta
Canada

DISCLAIMER:

This book contains the opinions and ideas of the author. The purpose of this book is to provide you with helpful information about business networking. This book should not be relied upon solely to grow your business network. Careful attention has been paid to ensure the accuracy of the information, but the author cannot assume responsibility for the validity or consequences of its use. This information is not intended to be all things to all business networkers. It is, by nature, generic, to business networking in general.

The material in this book is for informational purposes only. As each individual situation is unique, the author disclaims responsibility for any adverse effects that may result from the use or application of the information contained in this book. Any use of the information found in this book is the sole responsibility of the reader. Any suggestions found in this book are to be followed only after consultation with your own trusted business advisors.

DEDICATION

I dedicate this book to the inner demons and inner angels in all of us. Thank you to everyone who has so patiently guided me as I figured out what it means to me to network for business. This book is for you, whether you were the title of "Go-Giver" or follow the mantra of "Giver's Gain." I appreciate the lessons you have shared with me. I hope to be able inspire another generation of networkers who truly care!

Special mention to Bob Burg and John David Mann for their book, The Go-Giver. You both inspired me to become a better networker (and a better writer).

.

THE 7 DEADLY SINS OF NETWORKING

Welcome to a journey unlike any other in the realm of professional networking. The 7 Deadly Sins of Networking explores a unique perspective on networking, diving into the often-unspoken pitfalls that professionals encounter and the virtues that can lead to true networking success.

Why focus on the "deadly sins" in networking? Like the traditional seven deadly sins, these behaviors – often subtle and unnoticed – can significantly hinder our professional relationships and growth. They lurk in the shadows of our interactions, guiding us away from the authentic connections that form the cornerstone of meaningful networking.

In these pages, you will encounter seven sins: Pride, Envy, Gluttony, Lust, Anger, Greed, and Sloth. Each sin is paired with its redeeming virtue: Humility, Gratitude, Temperance, Chastity, Patience, Generosity, and Diligence. Through a series of compelling narratives, we will explore how these sins manifest in professional settings and how embracing their corresponding virtues can transform our networking approach.

My own journey in the networking world, filled with trials and triumphs, inspired me to write this book. I have witnessed these sins and virtues in action and experienced firsthand the profound impact they can have on one's career and personal growth. This book is an invitation for you to reflect on your networking practices, to recognize where you might be inadvertently succumbing to these sins, and to discover the power of their virtues.

Expect to find not only stories but also practical insights and strategies that you can apply in your professional life. Each chapter is designed to offer a blend of narrative storytelling and actionable advice, ensuring a reading experience that is both enlightening and engaging.

As you turn these pages, I encourage you to reflect on your experiences in networking. Think about the times you have encountered these sins, in yourself or others, and consider how adopting the virtues could reshape your approach to professional relationships.

Let us embark on this journey together, uncovering the sins that hold us back and embracing the virtues that propel us forward. Welcome to a new understanding of networking – one that values authenticity, connection, and personal growth.

PRIDE

At the Cozy Café

In the heart of the bustling city, there was a café known for its serene ambiance, a stark contrast to the busy world outside. Its walls, adorned with vibrant art, echoed with the rich aroma of coffee. On a crisp autumn evening, this café became a meeting point for a unique reunion—a gathering of seven professionals, each embodying a different sin of networking. The air was filled with laughter and lively conversations as they reminisced and caught up.

As the night unfolded, the ambiance shifted from lighthearted banter to a more introspective tone. The group, recognizing a shared desire for growth, decided to delve into their personal journeys. They agreed to narrate their tales of transformation, each highlighting a particular sin and the virtue that helped them overcome it.

Patricia's Tale of Transformation

Patricia, with a self-assured smile, was the first to share. Once known for her commanding presence in the professional world, her journey from Pride to Humility was a tale of profound transformation.

In her early career, Patricia was the epitome of confidence, often tipping into arrogance. She was a natural leader but tended to dominate conversations, believing her insights were superior. Networking events were stages for her achievements, leaving little room for others.

The turning point came during a high-stakes project. Patricia's inability to value her team's input led to a disastrous outcome. This public failure was a humbling experience, revealing the limitations of her prideful approach. It was a moment that sparked a deep self-reflection.

Gradually, Patricia embraced Humility. She learned the art of listening and began to genuinely value others' perspectives. This shift from speaking to engaging transformed her approach to networking, fostering deeper connections and collaboration.

With Humility, Patricia's network blossomed. She formed relationships based on mutual respect and understanding, far richer than her previous connections. Her story concluded with insightful wisdom, "Once, my Pride isolated me; Humility has since connected me deeply with others."

As Patricia's story ended, the group reflected on her transformation, finding parallels in their own experiences. Her journey underscored the balance between confidence and Humility, a crucial lesson in their collective networking endeavors.

The group raised their cups in a toast to continuous learning and growth, each member eager to share their own story of transformation in the world of networking.

ENVY

Ethan's Journey from the Shadows of Envy

As the reflective mood deepened in the cozy café, Ethan leaned forward, ready to share his story. His journey depicted a transformation from the debilitating grip of Envy to the liberating embrace of Gratitude in the world of networking.

Ethan's Tale of Realization

Ethan, with a contemplative glance, began his tale, revealing his struggle with Envy. Despite his hard work and dedication, he often felt overshadowed by his peers' apparent ease at networking and their seemingly effortless successes. This constant comparison brewed a storm of Envy within him, clouding his perception and hindering his ability to appreciate his own journey and strengths.

He vividly recalled moments of resentment as he watched colleagues celebrate their achievements. His Envy was a barrier, isolating him and obstructing the formation of meaningful connections. He was fixated on what others had, neglecting the opportunities and strengths he possessed.

The turning point for Ethan was an eye-opening encounter at a networking event. He witnessed a colleague he envied, being lauded not just for their success but also for their Generosity and spirit of collaboration. This moment illuminated the destructive nature of his Envy and ignited a desire for change.

Ethan embarked on a path to embrace Gratitude. He began to actively appreciate others' achievements, extending congratulations and seeking to learn from their experiences. This shift in perspective unveiled the value in celebrating collective successes and in recognizing his own unique contributions.

As he practiced Gratitude, Ethan's network started to grow in depth and quality. He found joy in collaborative achievements and realized that by appreciating others, he was also valuing himself more. His networking approach transformed, becoming more about connection and less about comparison.

Concluding his story, Ethan shared a poignant insight, "Envy blinded me to the richness around me. Gratitude opened my eyes to my own worth and the value of others." His journey from Envy to Gratitude enriched not just his professional life but also brought a deeper sense of personal fulfillment.

The group listened, nodding in understanding, each recognizing the shadow of Envy in their own experiences. They discussed how easy it was to fall into the trap of comparison and how transformative it was to step into the light of Gratitude.

Ethan's story added another layer to the tapestry of their shared experiences, emphasizing the power of Gratitude in transforming not just networking approaches but personal outlooks as well.

GLUTTONY

Greg's Shift from Overindulgence to Mindfulness

As the tales unfolded in the tranquil setting of the café, Greg readied himself to share his story, a narrative marking his transition from the excesses of Gluttony to the moderation of Temperance in networking.

Greg's Journey to Balance

Greg, with an air of earnestness, began recounting his early days in the networking world. He described himself as the quintessential networker, always present at every event, his pockets bulging with business cards. His approach was one of relentless pursuit, an insatiable appetite for connections, leading him to a path of networking Gluttony.

He vividly painted a picture of how this overindulgence led to a network that was vast yet shallow. Greg was a familiar face everywhere but lacked meaningful presence anywhere. This realization struck him hard – in his effort to be part of every circle, he had failed to forge deep, valuable connections.

A moment of introspection came after a period of burnout, a consequence of his non-stop networking spree. It was during a conversation with a seasoned networker that Greg encountered the concept of Temperance in networking – the idea of being selective and purposeful in his interactions.

Embracing this new approach, Greg began to choose his networking events with care, focusing on quality rather than quantity. This change led him to foster deeper connections, invest time in nurturing relationships, and engage more genuinely. Networking became less about collecting contacts and more about building meaningful relationships.

Greg concluded his story with a reflective note, "In Temperance, I discovered the true essence of networking. It is about the depth of your connections, not just the number." His journey from Gluttony to Temperance reshaped his networking philosophy, emphasizing the importance of meaningful and mindful connections.

The group, resonating with Greg's experiences, discussed the common pitfalls of networking Gluttony. They shared insights into the value of Temperance, finding a balance that enriches both professional and personal aspects of networking.

Greg's tale added a crucial dimension to the evening's discourse, underscoring the importance of intentionality and depth in building a sustainable and rewarding network.

LUST

Lucy's Transition from Unbridled Ambition to Sincere Connections

The atmosphere in the café, rich with stories of transformation, turned towards Lucy. Her tale was one of shifting from the intense desires of Lust in her networking efforts to the virtue of Chastity, characterized by genuine intentions and modesty.

Lucy's Path to Authenticity

Lucy began her story with a reflection on her early career, marked by an aggressive pursuit of success. She described her ambition as an unbridled longing for rapid advancement and recognition. This approach to networking was driven by a Lust for achievements, often leading to transactional relationships devoid of sincerity and depth.

She recounted how her relentless chase for success often overshadowed the true purpose of networking. Her interactions were more about leveraging connections for personal gain than about building mutual support and genuine relationships. This pursuit of success, she realized, was leaving her with a network that was extensive yet superficial.

The turning point for Lucy came with a significant professional setback. An important deal, which she had pursued with her usual fervor, fell through, not because of its merits but due to her reputation for being overly aggressive and self-serving. This moment of failure was a revelation, revealing the hollowness of her approach and prompting a revaluation of her networking style.

Embracing the virtue of Chastity, Lucy transformed her approach to networking. She began to engage with her peers with sincerity and Humility, focusing on fostering authentic, mutually beneficial relationships. This shift from a success-at-all-costs mentality to one of genuine engagement brought a newfound depth to her professional interactions.

Lucy concluded her story with a profound insight, "In Chastity, I discovered the real value of networking – not in the immediate gains, but in the lasting connections we build." Her journey from lustful ambition to sincere networking redefined her understanding of success, emphasizing the importance of authenticity and genuine connections.

The group listened intently, recognizing elements of Lucy's struggle in their own experiences. They discussed the challenges of maintaining integrity in professional ambitions and the rewards of embracing authenticity in networking.

Lucy's narrative added another layer to the evening's shared wisdom, highlighting the transformative power of sincerity and modesty in professional relationships and networking success.

ANGER

Arthur's Overcoming of Anger with Patience

As the stories continued to weave a tapestry of change and growth, Arthur prepared to share his tale. His was a journey of overcoming the fiery grips of Anger in networking and discovering the calming strength of Patience.

Arthur's Transformation

Arthur started his story with a candid acknowledgment of his past, marked by a quick temper and impatience. His professional life was riddled with instances where minor irritations or disagreements would quickly escalate due to his fiery responses. This approach often led to strained relationships and missed opportunities, casting a shadow on his otherwise expert reputation.

He shared a turning point that struck a chord with him deeply. During a pivotal networking event, an intense argument with a key contact led to a significant loss, a reminder that his Anger was more of a hindrance than an asset. This incident was a wake-up call, illuminating the destructive path his wrath had carved in his networking journey.

Embarking on a path to embrace Patience was challenging for Arthur. He began practicing active listening and mindfulness, learning to respond thoughtfully rather than reacting impulsively. He strived to understand first, to approach conflicts with a mindset of resolution and empathy, rather than contention.

This shift in approach brought a profound transformation in Arthur's professional relationships. Colleagues who had once been cautious became collaborative, recognizing the change in his demeanor. Patience allowed him to resolve conflicts effectively, leading to a more robust and cooperative network.

Arthur concluded his story, reflecting, "Adopting Patience did not just change my networking approach; it transformed my entire perspective. It turned potential conflicts into opportunities for growth and collaboration." His journey from Anger to Patience reshaped not only his professional interactions but also his personal outlook.

The group absorbed Arthur's story, recognizing their own moments of impatience and the wisdom in his transformation. They discussed how embracing Patience can turn networking challenges into opportunities for growth and deeper connections.

Arthur's story added a crucial understanding to the evening's narrative, highlighting the power of Patience in building effective and harmonious professional relationships.

GREED

George's Shift from Materialism to Generosity

In the intimate ambiance of the café, George took the stage to narrate his transformation. His story was about moving away from the Greed that once colored his networking efforts to embracing the virtue of Generosity.

George's Journey to Altruism

George began his tale by reflecting on his initial approach to networking, driven by a relentless pursuit of material gains. He was always seeking the next big deal, the next lucrative opportunity. His interactions, primarily motivated by personal benefit, often overlooked the genuine connection and mutual support aspects of networking.

He recalled a specific event that marked a turning point in his career. A potentially fruitful business partnership crumbled, not due to the lack of merit in the proposal, but because of his known reputation for being excessively self-centered. This incident was a stark realization that his Greed-driven approach was limiting, rather than advancing, his professional relationships.

The transition to embracing Generosity was pivotal for George. He began to approach his network with the intention to give rather than receive. He focused on contributing to the success of his contacts, sharing his time, resources, and expertise, without an immediate expectation of return.

This change in perspective brought about a significant shift in his professional life. George's network started to flourish in ways it never had before. By prioritizing Generosity, he built a network based on mutual respect and trust, leading to more fulfilling and sustainable success.

George concluded his story with a reflective insight, "In Generosity, I found the true essence of success – not in material gains, but in the richness of my relationships." His journey from Greed to Generosity redefined his approach to networking, highlighting the profound impact of selflessness and mutual support.

The group listened intently, drawing lessons from George's experience. They shared their thoughts on the often-overlooked power of Generosity in professional relationships and how it can lead to deeper, more meaningful connections.

George's story added another dimension to the evening's shared wisdom, underscoring the importance of Generosity in fostering a supportive and thriving professional network.

SLOTH

Samantha's Emergence from Inaction to Engagement

As the evening at the café drew towards a close, Samantha shared her story, a narrative about her evolution from the passive inactivity of Sloth in networking to the active commitment of Diligence.

Samantha's Path to Proactive Networking

Samantha began her tale by describing her initial approach to networking: one marked by avoidance and passivity. She preferred the comfort of familiar routines, steering clear of the efforts and challenges involved in active networking. This slothful approach led to missed opportunities and a stagnation in her professional growth.

She recounted an incident that served as a catalyst for change. A highly coveted role at her company slipped through her fingers, not due to a lack of skills, but because she had not built the necessary connections. This missed chance was a stark reminder of the importance of active engagement and the pitfalls of complacency in networking.

Motivated by this realization, Samantha embarked on a journey to embrace Diligence. She began to attend industry events, not just as an observer but as an active participant. She set goals for networking, held herself accountable, and steadily built a robust network through consistent effort and genuine interaction.

The transformation in her networking approach yielded tangible results. Opportunities that were once out of reach began to materialize, and her network grew in both size and quality. More importantly, she found a newfound sense of fulfillment and purpose in the connections she nurtured.

Reflecting on her journey, Samantha shared, "In embracing Diligence, I unlocked the true potential of networking – it's about presence and engagement, not just attendance." Her transition from Sloth to Diligence not only expanded her professional network but also instilled a deeper appreciation for the value of active participation.

The group, inspired by Samantha's story, reflected on the importance of proactive engagement in networking. They discussed the common tendency to underestimate the effort required in building effective networks and the rewards of diligent, purposeful interaction.

Samantha's narrative concluded the series of transformations, emphasizing the collective learning and growth experienced by the group. They left the café that evening enriched by each other's journeys, each story a testament to the diverse paths in mastering the art of networking.

EMBRACING VIRTUES

As we reach the end of our journey through "The 7 Deadly Sins of Networking," it is time to reflect on the profound lessons we have encountered. This book was not just about understanding the pitfalls that can ensnare us in our professional interactions; it was about discovering the path to a more fulfilling, effective, and genuine way of connecting with others.

THE PATH TO TRANSFORMATION

Each sin we explored – Pride, Envy, Gluttony, Lust, Anger, Greed, and Sloth – represents common traps that can easily entangle us in the complex web of professional networking. However, with each sin, we found a beacon of hope in its corresponding virtue – Humility, Gratitude, Temperance, Chastity, Patience, Generosity, and Diligence. These virtues are not just antidotes to the sins; they are guiding lights leading us to a richer, more rewarding networking experience.

THE POWER OF SELF-REFLECTION

As you read the stories of Patricia, Ethan, Greg, Lucy, Arthur, George, and Samantha, you likely saw reflections of your own professional journey. Perhaps you recognized moments where you faltered, succumbed to one of these sins, or maybe you recalled times when you embodied these virtues. This self-reflection is the first step towards meaningful change.

NETWORKING AS A COMMUNITY ENDEAVOR

Remember, effective networking is not just about advancing our careers or expanding our professional circle; it is about building a community. It is about forging connections that are not just beneficial but also supportive, nurturing, and enriching. Each virtue we embrace in our networking efforts helps us contribute to a community that is grounded in mutual respect, shared growth, and collective success.

LOOKING FORWARD

As you move forward in your networking journey, I encourage you to carry the lessons from this book with you. Approach each interaction with mindfulness, considering not just what you can gain, but also what you can contribute. Embrace Humility, express Gratitude, practice Temperance, engage with sincerity, respond with Patience, give generously, and pursue your goals diligently.

THE JOURNEY CONTINUES

Our journey through the 7 deadly sins of networking may have concluded, but your personal journey of growth and improvement continues. Armed with the insights from this book, you are now better equipped to navigate the complex world of professional networking, turning potential pitfalls into stepping stones for success.

Thank you for joining me on this enlightening journey. May your path be filled with rewarding connections, genuine relationships, and endless opportunities for growth and success.

KEY TAKEAWAYS

These key takeaways are designed to facilitate self-reflection and encourage readers to apply the lessons from each story to their professional and personal lives.

Pride (Patricia's Story)

- Overconfidence and arrogance in networking can isolate you from meaningful connections.
- Humility fosters deeper, more respectful, and collaborative relationships.
- The balance between confidence and Humility is crucial for effective networking.

Envy (Ethan's Story)

- Envy can blind you to your own strengths and hinder genuine connections.
- Gratitude shifts the focus from comparison to appreciation, enhancing personal and professional growth.
- Celebrating others' successes can lead to a more fulfilling and collaborative networking experience.

Gluttony (Greg's Story)

- Networking without purpose can lead to superficial connections and burnout.
- Temperance in networking means being selective and purposeful, leading to deeper relationships.
- Quality of connections is more important than quantity in building a meaningful network.

Lust (Lucy's Story)

- Pursuing networking with an aggressive, gain-driven mentality can lead to shallow relationships.
- Sincerity and modesty in networking foster genuine, mutually beneficial connections.
- Authentic engagement in networking is more rewarding than pursuing immediate gains.

Anger (Arthur's Story)

- Anger and impatience in networking can damage relationships and close off opportunities.
- Patience allows for better understanding and effective conflict resolution, enhancing professional interactions.
- Embracing Patience in networking leads to more respectful and collaborative relationships.

Greed (George's Story)

- A networking approach driven by self-interest and material gains can lead to superficial connections.
- Generosity in networking fosters deeper, more trusting relationships and mutual success.
- Valuing relationships over material gains enriches both professional and personal life.

Sloth (Samantha's Story)

- Passive, reactive networking can result in missed opportunities and hinder professional growth.
- Active, diligent engagement in networking leads to more opportunities and deeper connections.

- The effort invested in proactive networking pays off in terms of career advancement and personal satisfaction.

JOURNALING PROMPTS

These journaling prompts are designed to facilitate self-reflection and encourage readers to apply the lessons from each story to their professional and personal lives.

Pride (Patricia's Story)

- Reflect on a time when someone's prideful behavior affected you negatively. How did it make you feel?
- Consider a moment when someone's Humility positively impacted you. What difference did it make in your interaction?
- Recall an instance where you may have let Pride influence your networking approach. How could Humility have changed the outcome?
- Identify a moment you demonstrated Humility in a professional setting. What was the result?
- List actionable steps you can take to incorporate Humility into your networking strategy.

Envy (Ethan's Story)

- Reflect on a situation where you felt envious of someone's networking success. How did it impact your feelings towards them and yourself?
- Recall a time when someone expressed genuine Gratitude towards you. How did that influence your relationship?
- Think about a moment when you might have let Envy affect your professional behavior. What would have been different if you approached it with Gratitude?

- Remember an instance where you felt grateful for someone else's achievements. How did it change your perspective?
- Write down ways you can practice Gratitude in your professional life to overcome feelings of Envy.

Gluttony (Greg's Story)

- Think about a time when someone's excessive networking (quantity over quality) affected your perception of them. How did it influence your interaction?
- Consider an experience where someone's selective and meaningful approach to networking made a positive impression on you. What did you learn from it?
- Reflect on a moment where you might have prioritized quantity over quality in networking. How could a more tempered approach have been more effective?
- Recall an instance where you practiced Temperance in networking. What was the outcome?
- Identify specific actions you can take to ensure your networking efforts are more focused and purposeful.

Lust (Lucy's Story)

- Reflect on a situation where someone's aggressive pursuit of success in networking affected your relationship with them. How did it make you feel?
- Recall a time when someone's genuine and humble approach in a professional setting positively impacted you. What was the significance of that interaction?

- Think about an instance where your ambition may have overshadowed the importance of genuine connections. How could a more sincere approach have altered the outcome?
- Remember a moment when you engaged authentically in a networking opportunity. What were the results?
- Write down steps you can take to ensure your networking efforts are driven by sincerity and genuine interest.

Anger (Arthur's Story)

- Reflect on a time when someone's Anger or impatience in a professional setting impacted you negatively. How did you feel?
- Recall a situation where someone's Patience in resolving a conflict made a positive difference. What did you learn from that experience?
- Think about a moment where your Anger or impatience might have affected a networking opportunity. How could Patience have changed the outcome?
- Identify an instance where you demonstrated Patience in a challenging professional situation. What was the result?
- List actionable steps you can take to cultivate Patience in your networking approach.

Greed (George's Story)

- Think about a time when someone's Greed or self-serving attitude in networking affected your perception of them. How did it influence your interaction?

- Recall a moment when someone's Generosity in a professional context positively impacted you. What difference did it make?

- Reflect on an instance where your actions in networking may have been driven by self-interest. How could a more generous approach have benefited the situation?

- Remember a time when you acted generously in a networking context. What were the outcomes?

- Write down ways you can practice Generosity in your professional interactions to build more meaningful relationships.

Sloth (Samantha's Story)

- Reflect on a situation where someone's passive approach to networking impacted your relationship or opportunity. How did it affect your interaction?

- Think about a time when someone's active and engaged networking approach impressed you. What did you take away from that experience?

- Recall an instance where your passive approach to networking might have cost you an opportunity. How could Diligence have altered the outcome?

- Identify a moment when you actively engaged in a networking opportunity. What were the results?

- List actionable steps you can take to be more proactive and diligent in your networking efforts.

DISCUSSION GROUP

These questions are designed to stimulate thoughtful discussions in a group setting, encouraging participants to reflect on their current networking practices and consider the benefits of embracing the corresponding virtues.

Pride to Humility

- How might embracing Humility in your networking efforts enrich your professional relationships?
- What personal values could be better reflected by practicing Humility?
- Can you recall a moment when someone's Humility positively impacted you?
- How would your network change if you approached interactions with more Humility?
- What are the potential benefits of being more receptive and less dominant in conversations?
- In what ways might Humility contribute to your long-term networking success?

Envy to Gratitude

- How could expressing Gratitude towards others' successes enrich your own networking experience?
- What might you gain personally and professionally by shifting your focus from Envy to appreciation?
- How does feeling envious affect your emotional well-being compared to feeling grateful?
- Can you think of a situation where showing Gratitude could have improved a professional relationship?
- What are the potential benefits of fostering a mindset of Gratitude in your networking approach?

- How might recognizing and celebrating others' achievements positively impact your career?

Gluttony to Temperance

- What changes could you expect in your networking outcomes by focusing on deeper, more meaningful connections?
- How might being more selective and intentional in networking events enhance your professional life?
- What would be the impact on your personal well-being by adopting a more balanced approach to networking?
- How could practicing Temperance in networking reflect positively on your professional image?
- What might you gain by investing more time in fewer but more significant relationships?
- In what ways could a tempered approach to networking align with your long-term career goals?

Lust to Chastity

- How would your networking approach change if you prioritized genuine connections over immediate gains?
- What long-term benefits might you experience by adopting a more sincere and modest networking style?
- Can you recall a time when someone's authenticity in networking made a lasting impression on you?
- How could focusing on building honest relationships impact your professional reputation?

- What are the potential advantages of approaching networking with a mindset of mutual benefit?
- In what ways could authenticity in your networking interactions lead to more fulfilling outcomes?

Anger (Arthur's Story) to Patience

- How might practicing Patience improve your professional interactions and networking outcomes?
- Can you think of a situation where responding with Patience rather than Anger would have been more beneficial?
- What changes in your relationships could occur if you approached conflicts with Patience and understanding?
- How would a more patient approach to networking align with your personal values and professional ethos?
- What could be the long-term benefits for your career by being known as a patient and understanding professional?
- In what ways could practicing Patience impact your overall job satisfaction and career progression?

Greed to Generosity

- How could a shift from focusing on personal gains to generous giving enhance your networking effectiveness?
- What personal values might be better reflected by adopting a generous approach in your professional life?

- Can you think of a time when acting generously in a networking context would have benefitted both parties?
- How would your perception in your professional network change if you were more generous?
- What are the potential benefits, both personal and professional, of being seen as a generous and supportive networker?
- In what ways could practicing Generosity contribute to more meaningful and lasting professional relationships?

Sloth to Diligence

- How could adopting a more proactive and diligent approach to networking open up new opportunities for you?
- What might you achieve in your career by transitioning from a passive to an active networking style?
- Can you recall a missed opportunity due to inactivity? How could Diligence have changed the outcome?
- How would your professional life improve by regularly engaging in deliberate networking activities?
- What are the benefits of being actively involved in your professional community?
- In what ways could a diligent approach to networking reflect positively on your professional reputation and achievements?

BOOK CLUB

We wanted to share some thought-provoking and open-ended questions to facilitate engaging discussions in your book club. Here are ten questions tailored for The 7 Deadly Sins of Networking, which can encourage insightful conversations in a book club setting:

- Reflecting on Personal Experiences: Which of the 7 deadly sins of networking resonated with you the most and why? Have you experienced any of these sins in your professional life?

- Impact of Virtues: How do you think practicing the corresponding virtues can change one's professional networking approach? Can you share an example from your own experience?

- Character Analysis: Which character's story did you find most compelling or relatable, and what lessons did you draw from their transformation?

- Application of Themes: How can the themes of Humility, Gratitude, Temperance, Chastity, Patience, Generosity, and Diligence be applied in today's networking world?

- Personal Growth: After reading the book, have you identified any aspects of your networking approach that you would like to change? What specific steps do you plan to take?

- Favorite Narratives: Which story or sin/virtue pair did you find most engaging, and what about it stood out to you?

- Real-World Relevance: How do you think the concepts discussed in the book apply to real-world networking scenarios? Can these virtues realistically counteract the sins in a professional setting?

- Author's Perspective: What do you think was the author's main intention or message in writing this book? How effectively do you think they conveyed it?
- Comparative Analysis: Compare and contrast two different sins and their corresponding virtues discussed in the book. How do they differently impact networking success?
- Actionable Insights: What are some actionable insights or strategies from the book that you can implement in your networking approach? How do you plan to integrate these into your professional life?

JOIN THE SINNERS AND SAINTS NETWORKING CLUB

As you turn the final page of "The 7 Deadly Sins of Networking," your journey does not have to end here. In fact, a new chapter awaits you – one that involves becoming part of a vibrant, engaging, and supportive community. We invite you to join the Sinners and Saints Networking Club on LinkedIn, a community dedicated to transforming the way we network, one connection at a time.

What to Expect in the Community:

- Continuous Learning: Just like the stories and lessons in the book, our community is a space for ongoing learning and development. Engage in discussions, share insights, and gain new perspectives on effective networking.

- Real-World Application: Apply the virtues of Humility, Gratitude, Temperance, Chastity, Patience, Generosity, and Diligence in real-world scenarios. Share your experiences and learn how others are integrating these principles into their professional lives.

- Supportive Network: Connect with like-minded professionals who are also on a journey to improve their networking skills. Find mentors, collaborators, and friends who can support you in your professional growth.

- Interactive Challenges and Activities: Participate in challenges and activities designed to help you practice the virtues in practical, everyday situations.

- Expert Guidance: Gain insights from industry experts, join webinars, and participate in Q&A sessions to deepen your understanding of effective networking.
- Community Engagement: Share your successes and challenges, ask for advice, and offer your support to others. This club is about mutual growth and collective success.

Your Next Step in Networking Excellence

Joining the Sinners and Saints Networking Club is more than just being part of a group; it is about being part of a movement that values authentic, meaningful, and effective networking. It is a place where the lessons from the book come to life, and where you can continue to grow, learn, and succeed.

We cannot wait to welcome you into our community. Together, let us turn networking sins into networking wins!

You can learn more by visiting us at

https://www.globalwellnesshq.com/sinners-and-saints-networking-club

www.ingramcontent.com/pod-product-compliance
Lightning Source LLC
Chambersburg PA
CBHW060010300526
45794CB00003B/1160